What Are the Chances?

by Jennifer Prescott

STECK-VAUGHN
Harcourt Supplemental Publishers

www.steck-vaughn.com

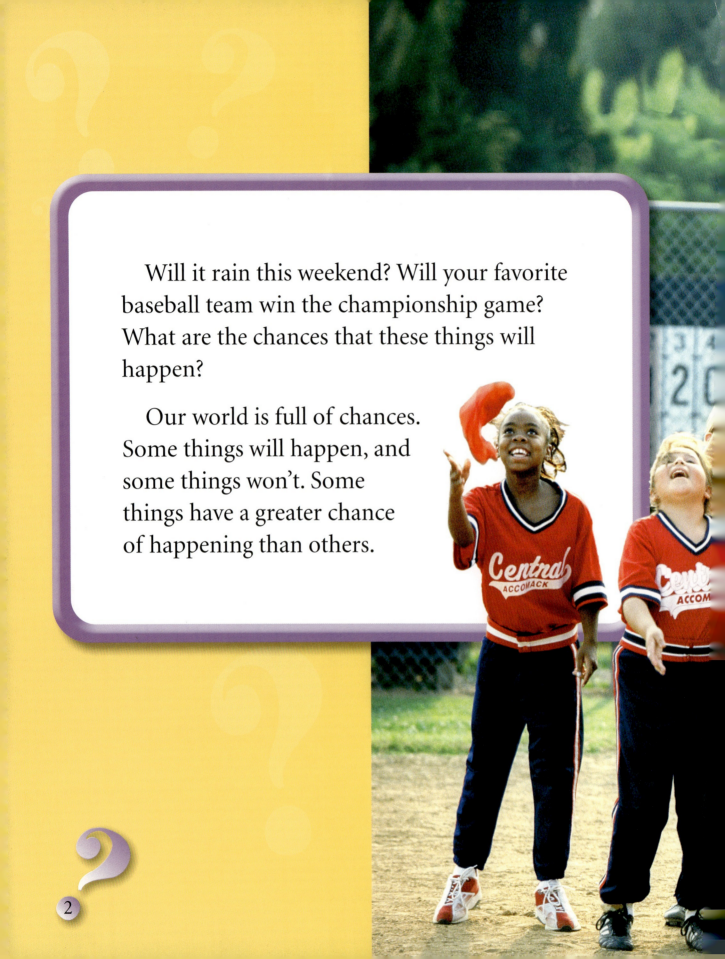

Will it rain this weekend? Will your favorite baseball team win the championship game? What are the chances that these things will happen?

Our world is full of chances. Some things will happen, and some things won't. Some things have a greater chance of happening than others.

Some things are **certain.** We know they will happen. It is certain that the sun will come up in the morning. It is certain that you will be a day older tomorrow than you are today.

Some things are **impossible.** We know that they could never happen. Time could never go backwards. Adults could never become babies again. A tree could never shrink back into a seed.

By knowing what is certain and what is impossible, we can **make predictions** about what **might** happen. A prediction is a good guess based on what you already know.

Some predictions are easy to make. What kind of babies will a dog have? It will have puppies, of course! It is certain that a dog's babies will be puppies. Could a dog's babies ever be kittens? No! That would be impossible.

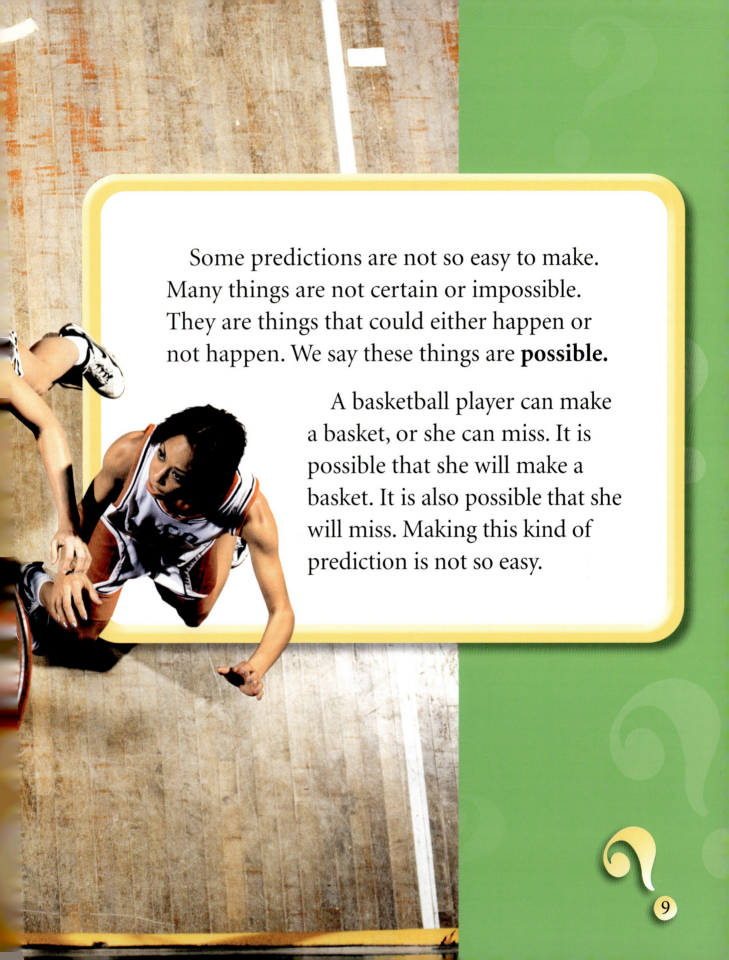

Some predictions are not so easy to make. Many things are not certain or impossible. They are things that could either happen or not happen. We say these things are **possible.**

A basketball player can make a basket, or she can miss. It is possible that she will make a basket. It is also possible that she will miss. Making this kind of prediction is not so easy.

On a cloudy day, it is possible that it could rain. We might say that there is a good **chance** of rain. We may decide to wear a raincoat or carry an umbrella.

Even on a very cloudy day, it is not certain that it will rain. It is also possible that the sun will come out and the clouds will disappear. Predicting the weather can be tricky!

The more we know about something, the easier it is to predict what will happen. If a gumball machine is full of only **blue** gumballs, what color gumball will you get?

If a gumball machine is full of **blue** gumballs, you are certain to get a **blue** gumball. There is no chance of getting any other color.

What if there is more than one color of gumball in the gumball machine? If the machine has both **blue** gumballs and **red** gumballs, do you know which color you will get?

With more than one color of gumball, you can't be certain which color you will get. You could get a **blue** gumball or a **red** one. But more information can help you make a prediction.

If you know there are **35 red** gumballs and **10 blue** gumballs in the machine, you can make a prediction. Which color gumball are you **more likely** to get?

There are more **red** gumballs than **blue** gumballs. So you are more likely to get a **red** gumball than a **blue** one. The chances of getting a **red** gumball are greater than the chances of getting a **blue** one.

Knowing the number of things can help you make predictions. There are **7 blue** marbles and **13 green** marbles shown here. If you choose a marble without looking, which color are you **less likely** to choose?

The number of **blue** marbles is less than the number of **green** marbles. So you are less likely to choose a **blue** marble.

Let's make some more predictions! There are **2 apples, 1 peach,** and **4 oranges** on this plate of fruit. If you choose a piece of fruit without looking, which kind are you **most likely** to choose?

There are more oranges than either apples or peaches on this plate. So you are most likely to pick an orange. The chances of picking an orange are greater than the chances of picking an apple or a peach.

There are three kinds of cookies on this plate. There are **4 chocolate chip** cookies, **6 peanut butter** cookies, and **5 sugar** cookies. If you choose a cookie without looking, which kind are you **least likely** to choose?

The number of chocolate chip cookies is less than the number of either peanut butter or sugar cookies. So you are least likely to choose a chocolate chip cookie. Let's hope that chocolate chip isn't your favorite!

Making predictions can be easy if you have the right information. You can use what you know to decide if something is certain, impossible, most likely, or least likely.

Could a butterfly ever become a caterpillar again? What do you predict? What are the chances?